# Starting
# Secondary School
# *English*

First published 2002
exclusively for WHSmith by

Hodder & Stoughton Educational
338 Euston Road
London
NW1 3BH

A CIP record for this book is available from the British
Library.

Text: Louis Fidge

Typeset by Fakenham Photosetting Ltd, Fakenham, Norfolk.

ISBN 0 340 84735 2

Printed and bound in Spain by Graphycems.

# Contents

# Introduction

The move from primary to secondary school can be quite an overwhelming experience. You will encounter completely new subject areas and a whole range of new topics and concepts, as well as new teachers and a new and much bigger school environment. Some people say it is like changing from a big fish in a small pond (primary school) into a small fish in a big pond (secondary school)!

The books in this *Starting Secondary School* series will help bridge the gap between primary and secondary school and ease the transition between the two.

## From a big fish in a small pond to a small fish in a big pond.

This introduction will answer some of the most frequently asked questions about starting secondary school.

## What are lessons like at secondary school?

You'll probably be placed in a tutor group, which meets for registration each day with the same teacher, and you are likely to stay with this group for quite a few subjects. In some subjects, like English and maths, you may be placed in a set with other children of similar ability to make it easier for you and the rest to work at a similar pace.

The timetable is very important at secondary school. Lessons are for set times and there may be a bell signalling the end of each lesson. Different subjects are taught in different rooms and you will be told and shown where to go. It is important to get to know your timetable as quickly as possible and to know where to go for each lesson. You could fill in the blank timetable at the end of this book to help you.

## Will I be able to find my way around?

Life at secondary school may seem very different to life at primary school at first. For a start, everything seems much bigger. The buildings are bigger, the students are bigger – and there are more of them! A common fear is of getting lost or not being able to find your way around. Don't worry. Your teachers will make sure you know where to go and there's always someone you can ask. Remember – if in doubt about anything, ask! Nobody will mind if you do. Everyone at the school is there to help you, and to help you to do your best.

## How do secondary schools work?

Each subject follows a scheme of work, which has been agreed by each subject department and will be based on Key Stage 3 of the National Curriculum. You will mostly study the same subjects you did at primary school. The main difference is that you will have different teachers to help you. You will also begin to study at least one modern foreign language, usually French or German. The choice of languages available differs from school to school.

## What about tests?

It is likely that you will have more tests and assessments at secondary school than you did at primary school. You will usually be told when these are to take place and will be given plenty of time to revise and prepare for them. If you are sensible and do your homework, these tests should not worry you at all.

## What about homework?

Homework is set in accordance with an agreed timetable so that you will have different subjects to deal with on different evenings. In your first year this will not be too time-consuming. A good tip is to do your homework as soon as you can, rather than leave it till the last minute and rush it. And remember to take it to school with you on the day you are supposed to hand it in!

## How will I cope with the extra freedom that I will have at secondary school?

A lot of emphasis is placed on being independent and responsible in secondary school. Thinking ahead and being organised will help you a lot. Always get to your lessons and take everything you need with you. The teachers will tell you what you need to bring to each lesson.

## How will my parents know what I am doing at school?

Most schools use a homework diary in which homework is recorded and some schools ask parents to sign these regularly to show that they have read them. It is important that your parents know what your are doing at school. This is one way of helping them find out. Don't forget to talk to them too! Your school will probably also have regular open evenings when your parents will be invited to school to talk to your teachers and discuss your progress.

## What will English be like at secondary school?

At primary school you will have been familiar with English being taught largely during the Literacy Hour. At secondary school you will study many of the same sorts of things at an appropriate level.

- You will read class novels, poetry and plays and study them.
- You will undertake all sorts of different pieces of writing – including stories, poetry, writing accounts, writing notes etc.
- You will study grammar, how to punctuate sentences and how language works.
- You will be expected to write neatly and quickly and spell well.
- You will learn how to take notes and use them effectively, and set your writing out logically.
- You will be taught how to plan and draft work, and improve and refine it.
- You will be expected to be able to use reference books, such as a dictionary and thesaurus.

## How will this book help me?

All of the things in this book are designed to help you with work you will be doing at secondary school in English. Work through the units in any order you wish. In the Glossary at the back of this book there is also a list of useful words used in English and their definitions.

**Good luck!**

# Looking carefully at words

**?**

## Which fits?

Which of these words will take the letter pattern **ea**? Which will take the letter pattern **oa**? Which will take both?

r___d

h___ven

m___ning

br___d

___ts

w___pon

___r

oc___n

b___st

c___l

*Which fits?*

## Looking for small words

Sometimes you will find small words inside longer words.

How many small words can you find in:

because?

anywhere?

shallow?

island?

tomatoes?

## Look for common letter patterns

**When spelling it is helpful to look for common letter patterns:**

catch, pitch, hutch.

## Try this . . .

Find and underline all the tch words in this list of jobs to be done.

> Watch the big match on TV.
> Fetch my sketchbook from upstairs.
> Stitch a patch on my jeans.
> Buy some plasters for scratches and itches.
> Get some ketchup from the kitchen.
> Feed my rabbit in the hutch.
> Mend the broken latch and broken catch.
> Switch off the lights at bedtime.

## Using known patterns to spell other words

**Once you know a common letter pattern, it may help you spell other words.**

## Try these . . .

What new words can you make if you:

★ change the c in care to b, d, r, sc, st, gl, bew, prep?

★ change the h in here to w, m, wh, th?

★ change the f in fire to h, w, t, d, m, sp, sh, requ?

★ change the m in more to b, c, w, t, sc, st, sn, bef?

★ change the p in pure to c, s, l, inj, sec, meas, pleas, treas?

# Pattern puzzler

Can you sort the words in the word wall into sets according to their common letter patterns? (There are three words in each set.)

| tough | learn | hedge | furniture | nation | fourteen |
|---|---|---|---|---|---|
| | search | badge | education | fracture | through | smudge |
| creature | journey | early | instruction | cough | humour |

# Same letter pattern – but different sound!

Although letter patterns are extremely helpful, keep your wits about you and don't always rely on them. Read this poem to see why! The same letter pattern will not always sound the same.

> Beware of heard, a dreadful word
> That looks like beard and sounds like bird.
> And dead: it's said like bed, not bead –
> For goodness' sake don't call it 'deed'!
> Watch out for meat and great and threat,
> They rhyme with suite and straight and debt.

## Try it yourself ▼

Underline the common letter pattern in each set of words.

| maiden | paid | afraid | said |
|---|---|---|---|
| alarm | swarm | charming | farmer |
| wall | tallest | calling | shall |
| wine | machine | finer | spine |
| expensive | diver | five | thrives |
| shoes | goes | potatoes | heroes |

Which word in each set is pronounced differently?

**? Take a word!**

What word will you be left with if you take:

ear from feared?
art from starting?
now from snowing?
age from message?
act from practice?

Enough's enough!

**! Enough's enough!**

How many different ways can the ough be pronounced in these words:

cough, through, although, bought, enough, drought, tough, bough, plough, thought, through, trough

# Parts of speech – Nouns

All the words in our language can be divided into groups, known as 'parts of speech' (or 'word classes'). Each part of speech has a particular job to do in a sentence.

Nouns are naming words. A noun may be the name of a person, place or thing.

## Common nouns

A common noun is a general name of a person (a boy), a place (a library) or a thing (a book).

> A boy went into the library to borrow a book.

In the 'noun wall' below there are four common nouns relating to people, four names of places and four names of things. Can you spot them?

| teacher | harbour | apple | dentist |
|---------|---------|-------|---------|
| garage | hangar | bike | nurse |
| mug | bank | artist | ruler |

## Proper nouns

A proper noun is the particular name of a person (Mrs Jones), a place (London) or a thing (Tower Bridge).

> Mrs Jones walked across Tower Bridge in London.

The capital letters in these sentences have been missed. Can you see where they should go?

1. tom and sam went to the ritz cinema in milton keynes.
2. yesterday was wednesday, the last day of march.
3. roald dahl wrote james and the giant peach.

## Abstract nouns

Abstract nouns are names of things we can understand in our minds but cannot receive with our five senses, for example truth.

The thief told the truth in court.

Find the three abstract nouns hidden in the letters below.

**qwertdangery**

**puhonestytfg**

**xcpatiencev**

## Collective nouns

A collective noun is the name of a group of people or things, such as a band of musicians.

These pairs of collective nouns are all muddled up. Work out what they are.

1. a bunch of stamps     a collection of bananas
2. a flock of elephants     a herd of sheep
3. a swarm of stones     a pile of bees

**No sense in abstract nouns!**

You cannot touch, taste, see, hear or smell abstract nouns.

**Noun-testing**

If you are not sure whether a word is a noun or not, try putting 'a', 'an' or 'the' in front of it. If it makes sense, then the word is a noun.

'the' pancake     a noun

'a' went     not a noun

'an' unhappy     not a noun

**Noun-spotting**

You can sometimes tell if a word is a noun by the way it ends.

Here are some **common noun endings** to remember:

**-or**: doctor, actor

**-ment**: government, retirement

**-tion**: station, action

**-ness**: goodness, happiness

**-ism**: magnetism, heroism

**-ice**: advice, practice

# Using a dictionary

Dictionaries are valuable sources of information. You need to know how to use them effectively and efficiently.

## Alphabetical order

To make it easy to look up words, dictionaries are organised in alphabetical order. To look up a word, first look up words beginning with the first letter. You may then need to go on to the second, third or fourth letter until you find the word you're looking for.

## Try this . . .

Which order would the following words come in?
a) recall       report        rearm       redirect?
b) postpone     postgraduate  postdate    postcode?
c) supersonic   superfine     supervise   supernatural?

## Meanings

Dictionaries help you look up the meanings of unfamiliar words. Each word has its own definition.

## Try these . . .

Do you know the difference between these pairs of homophones? Use a dictionary to check them out.

awe/oar                    curb/kerb        faint/feint
stationary/stationery    freeze/frieze    pray/prey

## ? Hit or miss?

How quickly can you find different letters in your dictionary? Test yourself. Think of different letters. Practise finding the letter as quickly as possible. Learn whereabouts each letter comes, e.g. m comes in the middle, t comes towards the end etc. Give yourself 10 points for each direct hit, with marks deducted for a near miss, bad miss and way out!

Top tip

## ★ Guide words

To look up words fast, use the guide words at the top of each dictionary page. They tell you the first and last words on the page.

## Spellings

If you are uncertain how to spell a word – look it up!

## Try it yourself ▼

Read the clues and look up the spellings of these tricky words.

**The answers all contain double letters.**

| | |
|---|---|
| pro _ _ _ _ _ _ _ | a teacher in a university |
| nec _ _ _ _ _ _ | something that is needed |
| dis _ _ _ _ _ _ | to vanish from sight |
| rec _ _ _ _ _ _ | to speak well of |
| har _ _ _ _ _ _ | to pester and annoy |
| suc _ _ _ _ _ _ | to get on well |
| mar _ _ _ _ _ _ | wonderful |
| pos _ _ _ _ _ _ | something you own |

al'-fuh-bet

## Pronunciation

Dictionaries often show how a word is pronounced. The word may be written phonetically (i.e. spelt how it is said). The word is usually divided into syllables with a stress mark after a syllable that must be emphasised: alphabet (al'-fuh-bet)

## Try this . . .

Every time you come to a word you are unsure how to say, check its pronunciation in your dictionary.

## ★ Headwords

As a way of saving space, not every word is listed separately in a dictionary. For example, **goodness** may be found under **good**, and **breakage** under **break**. The words **good** and **break** are called headwords.

## ❗ Parts of speech

A good dictionary will tell you what part of speech a word is: **v** (verb), **n** (noun) etc.

## ★ Etymology

Sometimes a dictionary will also show where a particular word originated (came from):

samovar (Russia)

# More about nouns

## Just to confuse you!

★ Some nouns are **uncountable** and have only a single form: happiness, beef, sunlight.

★ Some singular nouns **look** plural: news, measles etc.

★ Some nouns are **always** plural and hardly ever have a singular meaning: scissors, trousers etc.

★ Some nouns are **spelt the same** in both the singular and plural: sheep, deer etc.

★ Some nouns don't stick to the rules opposite: roof – roofs; photo – photos.

## Remember!

Never use an apostrophe (') to form plurals. Lots of adults do – and they're wrong!

## Countable nouns

Countable nouns may be singular or plural.

Singular **means** one; plural **means** more **than one – one car** but lots of cars.

When we change a noun from the singular to the plural, **the** spelling **often** changes, **e.g. one hero, two heroes.**

## Work out some rules

Work out these rules to help you remember how the spelling of plural nouns changes. Try to think of another example to prove each rule. Use a dictionary to help you if necessary.

| Rules for changing singular nouns to plural | singular | plural |
|---|---|---|
| We just add 's' to most nouns. | dog | dogs |
| When a noun ends with a vowel plus 'y' we add ____. | day | days |
| When a noun ends with a consonant plus 'y' we change the 'y' to ____ and add ____. | lorry | lorries |
| When a noun ends with 's', 'x', 'ch' or 'sh' we add ____. | brush | brushes |
| When a noun ends with 'f' or 'fe' we change the 'f' or 'fe' to ____ and add ____. | loaf | loaves |
| When a noun ends with a consonant plus 'o' we often add ___. | volcano | volcanoes |
| When a noun ends with a vowel plus 'o' we add ___. | video | videos |

# Gender

Nouns may be classified according to their gender.

A noun may be:

⭐ masculine (male): boy

⭐ feminine (female): girl

Do you know the feminine form of:

son?        uncle?        nephew?        father?        bridegroom?

# Animals

Match up the feminine and masculine form of each of these animals.

| cow | goose | hind | mare | ewe |
|------|---------|------|-----|------|
| gander | stallion | bull | ram | hart |

Nouns may also be:

⭐ common (when it could refer to either male or female): child

⭐ neuter (when it is neither masculine nor feminine): table

# Try this ...

Write each noun in the correct column of the chart.
(There should be three nouns in each column.)

| nun | pupil | | duke | tap | doctor | friend |
|-----|-------|--|------|-----|--------|--------|
| hotel | grandmother | box | wizard | bachelor | bride | |

| masculine | feminine | common | neuter |
|-----------|----------|--------|--------|
|           |          |        |        |

## HELPFUL HINT

Many feminine words end with ess:

count (masculine) – countess (feminine);

god (masculine) – goddess (feminine).

## Other languages

In some other languages objects are given masculine or feminine gender, which sounds a little strange to us. For example, in French la table (the table) is said to be feminine, but le crayon (the pencil) is masculine!

## Male or female?

We refer to lifeless things as if they were masculine or feminine at times. For example, we sometimes talk about a car in the feminine gender (She goes very well) and refer to Old Father Time (masculine).

## Did you know...?

**Fascinating fact**
Did you know the feminine of a sultan is a sultana?!

13

# Counting syllables

**Break it up!**
When you say words, you can tap out the syllables to help you hear them. Each syllable is like a beat. Try it out to some rap music!

**Be a robot**

**Be a robot**
If you have trouble hearing where syllables come in words, say them in a jerky, staccato-like voice, like a robot: I will ex-ter-min-ate you!

**Use a dictionary**
Some dictionaries will show you how a word is broken down into syllables: remember re/mem/ber

## About syllables

Spelling involves speaking and listening, as well as looking at words carefully. Breaking longer words down into sound 'chunks' often helps us hear how a word should be spelt. When we say a word slowly we can break it down into smaller parts, called syllables: Each syllable must contain at least one vowel. win/dow (2 syllables); per/form/ance (3 syllables); nev/er/the/less (4 syllables).

## Try this . . .

Say each of the words below slowly. Tap out the syllables. Decide if each word in the word wall is made up of two, three or four syllables.

| insult | conductor | photography | hospital | modern |
| information | careless | furniture | thermometer | suspension |
| district | machinery | tennis | finishing | transport |
| exclude | helpful | astonishment | universe |

## Syllable sums

The first syllable of each word is one of the prefixes in the box. Choose the correct prefix and complete each sum.

| re | ·im | il | pre | pro | ex | con | en |

___ + po + lite + ly = _____     ___ + cess + ion = _____

___ + plan + a + tion = _____     ___ + log + ic + al = _____

___ + mem + ber + ing = _____     ___ + light + en = _____

___ + par + a + tion = _____     ___ + sid + er + ing = _____

# Limericks

Limericks are comic verses containing five lines.
They have a clear rhythm and rhyme pattern.
The first recorded limerick was written over a hundred years ago.
Read this limerick. Count the number of syllables in each line.

> There was a young man from Bengal,
> Who went to a fancy dress ball.
> He went, just for fun,
> Dressed up as a bun.
> A dog ate him up in the hall!

## Try it yourself

### Complete this limerick in your own words.

There was an old man with a beard,
Who said, 'It's just as I _____!
Four larks and a wren,
Two owls and a _____,
Have all built their _____ in my beard!'

## ? What's it called?

Words with just one syllable (like **beat**) are called **monosyllabic** (**mono** means one). Words with two or more syllables (like **super** and **syllable**) are called **polysyllabic** (**poly** means many).

*Did you know...?*

## ★ Haiku

Haikus are short poems that have a clear, regular syllable pattern. They paint a vivid picture, and look at ordinary things in a different or unusual way. They originated in Japan.

*The sun – a yellow balloon*
(5 syllables)
*Floating in the bright blue sky*
(7 syllables)
*On a summer day.*
(5 syllables)

# Parts of speech — Verbs

All the words in our language may be divided into groups, known as 'parts of speech' (or 'word classes'). Each part of speech has a particular job to do in a sentence.

## Verbs

A verb can be either:

★ a doing word, telling us the action performed by a noun:
The lady opened the door.

★ or a being word, telling us about the state of a noun:
The door was green.

## Verb tenses

Verbs may be written in different tenses. The tense of the verb shows when the action takes place (or will take place or has taken place).

**Present tense** – The present tense is used when the action is happening now:
I sing. I am singing.

**Past tense** – The past tense is used when the action took place in the past:
I sang. I was singing.

**Future tense** – The future tense is used when the action is going to happen:
I will sing. I am going to sing.

# Regular verbs

Regular verbs always follow a pattern. Complete the chart below:

| Present tense | Past tense | Future tense |
|---|---|---|
| I watch | I watched | I will watch |
| I jump | I | I |
| I smile | | |
| I laugh | | |

# Irregular verbs

You cannot simply add 'ed' to irregular verbs in the past tense. They do not follow a simple pattern. The verb itself changes in some way.

Fill in the past tense of the irregular verbs below.

| Present tense | Past tense | Future tense |
|---|---|---|
| I think | I _____ | I will think |
| I sing | I _____ | I will sing |
| I eat | I _____ | I will eat |
| I fly | I _____ | I will fly |

# Expect the unexpected!

!  **Handy hints**

1. When we add the suffix 'full' (meaning 'full of') to the end of words we drop one 'l' and write it as 'ful': care + full = careful.

2. When we use 'all' in front of a word as a prefix or at the end of a word as a suffix, we drop one 'l': all + ways = always; music + all = musical

★ **The long and the short of it**

Sometimes a vowel may have a **short** sound: c**a**p. Sometimes the same vowel may have a **long** sound: c**a̲**pe.

Add an **e** to the end of each word and change the short middle vowel into a long vowel sound.

mat__; gap__; sham__; kit__; din__; rip__; slim__; rob__; not__; cub__; plum__; cut__.

Our language is full of surprises – especially in spelling!

## Hard or soft?

Sometimes the same consonant may have a hard or soft sound: **c**at, **g**one (hard sound); i**c**e, **g**iant (soft sound).

## Try these . . .

**Say each of these words. Write if the c or g is hard or soft.**

giraffe (soft)   cut (_____)   grab (_____)   range (_____)

cell (_____)   golf (_____)   custard (_____)   pages (_____)

France (_____)   ignite (_____)   gymnast (_____)   cabin (_____)

grace (_____)   silence (_____)   sags (_____)   giant (_____)

code (_____)   princess (_____)   cape (_____)   gust (_____)

## Unexpected vowel sounds

Sometimes vowels don't sound how we expect them to!

## Try this . . .

Look for words in the word wall where: the **o** sounds like **u** (as in fr**o**nt)   the **i** sounds like **y** (as in milli**o**n) the **a** sounds like **o** (as in w**a**tch).

| inferior | one | million | money | brilliant |
|---|---|---|---|---|
| done | lovely | experience | memorial | wonderful |
| companion | above | barrier | stomach | champion |
| compass | honey | convenient | shovel | radiant |

## The warm worm!

Read these words and then complete the sentences, saying what you notice.

| | | | | |
|---|---|---|---|---|
| worm | warm | world | reward | swarm |
| worse | work | warn | warrant | worth |

When ar comes after w it is often pronounced _____.

When or comes after w it is often pronounced _____.

## Sh!

Sh!

Read these words:

| | |
|---|---|
| musician | official |
| gracious | delicious |
| politician | special |

What you notice about the sound of ci in them?

Now read these words:

| | | |
|---|---|---|
| essential | infectious | confidential |
| fictitious | ambitious | initial |

What do you notice about the sound of ti in them?

?

### Final vowels

The most common vowel at the end of a word is **e**, as in **handle**. The other vowels are less common. How many words can you think of that end with a vowel other than **e**
(like **anaconda**, **kiwi**, **dingo**, **emu**)?

Chips please, Chef!

### Chat to the chef at school

The letters **ch** may be pronounced in at least three different ways.
How many more words can you think of for each set?
chips  cheese (with a sound like a sneeze!)
chef  champagne (like a sh sound)
anchor  stomach (like a ck sound)

# More about verbs

**Two types of verb**

Two important types of verb are:

★ transitive verbs

★ intransitive verbs.

**Handy hints**

★ Every sentence must have a **subject** and a **verb**.
The dog (**subject**) barked (**verb**).

★ Some sentences also have an **object**. (The object is the **person** or thing affected by the **subject**.)
The referee (**subject**) blew (**verb**) his whistle (**object**).

**Take care!**

Some verbs may be used transitively or intransitively, depending on the context.
The girl rang the bell. (transitive verb)
The bell rang. (intransitive verb)

## Transitive verbs

A transitive **verb is** followed by an object. The action **of a transitive verb** does something to somebody (or something).

| Subject | Verb | Object |
|---------|------|--------|
| Aunt Bess | hugged | Tom. |
| The car | overtook | the lorry. |

## Try this . . .

Think of a suitable subject or object to complete each sentence below.

| Subject | Verb | Object |
|---------|------|--------|
| Squirrels | eat | _____. |
| The farmer | ploughed | _____. |
| The dog | chewed | _____. |
| _____ | scored | a goal. |
| _____ | married | the prince. |
| _____ | bakes | bread. |

## Intransitive verbs

An intransitive **verb has** no object. For example, you cannot shiver **someone, or** cough **someone.**

| Subject | Verb | No Object |
|---------|------|-----------|
| The wet child | shivered. | — |
| The old man | coughed. | — |

# Active and passive voice

A verb may have two voices. The voice of the verb may be:

★ active

★ or passive.

## Active voice

In the active voice the subject performs the actions:

The snooker player hit the ball.

The monkey jumped from the tree.

## Passive voice

In the passive voice the subject has the action done to it by someone or something else.

The cup was won by the school team.

The English Channel was swum by Captain Webb.

1. Say whether each verb is in the active (**A**) or passive (**P**) voice.

   a) The treasure was found by the pirate chief.   ( **P** )

   b) The lion chased the antelope.                  (___)

   c) The king put on his crown.                     (___)

   d) The mouse was chased by the cat.               (___)

2. The subject of each sentence below has been left out. Say who, or what, you think is the missing subject.

   a) The car was mended           (by a mechanic).

   b) The Earth was invaded        (_____).

   c) The parcel was delivered     (_____).

   d) The song was recorded        (_____).

! **Top tip**

Sentences using the passive voice usually say who did the action.

The tree was chopped down by a lumberjack.

? **Whodunnit?**

Sometimes a sentence using the passive voice may not say who or what does the action. You have to make a guess, based on the context:

The team was defeated.
(by their opponents)
The jewels were stolen.
(by the thief)

# Parts of speech – Pronouns

All the words in our language may be divided into groups, known as 'parts of speech' (or 'word classes'). Each part of speech has a particular job to do in a sentence.

## Pronouns

A pronoun is a word that takes the place of a noun.

## Types of pronoun

**Personal pronouns** – Personal pronouns are used for people or things.
Harry got told off when he [Harry] was late.
Here are some common personal pronouns:

I  me  you  he  him  she  her  it  we  us  you  they  them

## Try these . . .

Work out who or what each underlined personal pronoun stands for.
1. When Edward picked up the apple, he (Edward) ate it (the apple).
2. Sophie has a TV in her bedroom. She (_____) is always watching it (_____).
3. "I (_____) love music," said James.
4. "Come with us (_____)," Cara and Emily said.
5. The man wanted the trousers but they (_____) were too dear for him (_____).

**Possessive pronouns** – Possessive pronouns show who or what owns them. This is my bag not yours!
Here are some common possessive pronouns:

my  mine  your  yours  his  her  hers  its  our  ours  their  theirs

## Handy hint
The prefix 'pro' means 'in the place of'. So 'pronoun' literally means 'in the place of a noun'.

## Remember!
The possessive pronouns yours, hers, its, ours and theirs never have apostrophes!
The dog wagged it's tail.
(wrong)
The dog wagged its tail.
(correct)

Reflexive pronouns – Reflexive pronouns link back to the subject. I washed myself.
Here are some common reflexive pronouns:

> myself    yourself    himself    herself    itself
> ourselves    yourselves    themselves

Demonstrative pronouns – Demonstrative pronouns point out nouns. This is my new coat.
Here are some common demonstrative pronouns:

> this    that    these    those    them

## The three persons of pronouns

Pronouns may be either singular or plural. A piece of writing may be written in:

★ the 1st person when it is about ourselves: I (singular), we (plural)

★ the 2nd person when it is about you: you (may be singular or plural)

★ the 3rd person when it is about others: he, she, it (singular), they (plural)

## Try it yourself ▼

### Choose the correct pronoun to complete each sentence.

1. Last night, _____ began to snow. (3rd person singular)
2. Will _____ pass me that newspaper, please? (2nd person singular)
3. _____ love playing computer games. (1st person singular)
4. Sam called for Emma and then _____ went to the park. (3rd person plural)
5. Anna is untidy. _____ leaves her clothes everywhere. (3rd person singular)

## ★ Other types of pronouns

★ Interrogative pronouns ask questions: Who is next?

Common interrogative pronouns are: who? which? what? whose?

★ Relative pronouns link people or things already mentioned: The bike that I ride is silver.

Common relative pronouns are: who, which, whom, whose, that

★ Indefinite pronouns link people or things that are not definitely defined in number: Is anyone there?

Common indefinite pronouns are: anyone, someone, several, some, none, sometimes

# Synonyms and antonyms

## Use a thesaurus

Use a thesaurus to look up synonyms for words. A thesaurus is a book that gives lists of words with similar meanings. If you know the word that you need, but want to say it in a more interesting way, a thesaurus will provide you with a list of alternative words, or 'synonyms', for that word.

You will also often find antonyms for words listed in a good thesaurus.

## Overused words

A thesaurus will help you avoid using the same word over and over again. Words like 'got', 'said', 'nice' and 'good' are very overused in our writing.

## Believe it or not!

One class of children found 303 different words meaning 'to move'!

## What are synonyms?

Synonyms are words with similar meanings:

hot, boiling, scorching.

## Why use synonyms?

Using synonyms helps you make your writing more interesting and varied.

## Play a synonym game

How many pairs of rhyming words meaning to speak can you think of? Here are some to give you an idea:

mutter/stutter; cheer/jeer; titter/twitter.

## A synonym poem

Read this poem. It is full of synonyms.

Jibber, jabber, babble, gabble,
Cackle, clack and prate,
Twiddle, twaddle, mutter, stutter,
Utter, splutter, blate . . .

Chatter, patter, tattle, prattle,
Chew the rag and crack,
Spiel and spout and spit it out,
Tell the world and quack . . .

Sniffle, snuffle, drawl and bawl,
Snicker, snort and snap,
Bark and buzz and yap and yelp,
Chin and chirp and chat . . .

Shout and shoot and gargle, gasp,
Gab and gag and groan,
Hem and haw and work the jaw,
Grumble, mumble, moan.

## Synonym challenge

Think of a word of five letters that has a similar meaning to each of the words below. Use a thesaurus to help you.

a) velocity _ _ _ _ _       b) deceive _ _ _ _ _       c) brief _ _ _ _ _

d) infuriated _ _ _ _ _       e) coarse _ _ _ _ _       f) mistake _ _ _ _ _

g) compel _ _ _ _ _       h) diminutive _ _ _ _ _       i) despise _ _ _ _ _

# What is an antonym?

An antonym is a word meaning the opposite: Antonyms for hot could be cold, icy, freezing, bleak, raw etc.

# Prefix puzzler

Use a dictionary to help you find as many words as possible that can be given the opposite meaning by adding each of the following prefixes:

> un-    dis-    in-    ir-    il-    im-    non-

# Antonym challenge

Think of a word of five letters that has the opposite meaning to each of the words below.

a) clean _ _ _ _ _
b) lost _ _ _ _ _
c) noisy _ _ _ _ _
d) war _ _ _ _ _
e) friend _ _ _ _ _
f) late _ _ _ _ _
g) full _ _ _ _ _
h) long _ _ _ _ _
i) true _ _ _ _ _

**? Do all words have antonyms?**
No! For example, can you think of an antonym for yellow or at?

**★ Change the suffix**
We can give some words the opposite meaning by changing their suffixes: careful – careless.

**★ Prefixes and antonyms**
We can make some words mean the opposite by adding a prefix:
wise – unwise;
agree – disagree;
sane – insane;
movable – immovable;
legal – illegal;
reverent – irreverent;
sense – nonsense

# Parts of speech — Adjectives

All the words in our language may be divided into groups, known as 'parts of speech' (or 'word classes'). Each part of speech has a particular job to do in a sentence.

## Adjectives

Adjectives are describing words. They give us more information about nouns (or pronouns): a loud noise; Lucky you!

## Different types of adjective

★ **Descriptive adjectives**

The most common adjectives are descriptive adjectives. They describe things. Find the descriptive adjective in each set of letters below.

qwerclevertu    oplkjheavybn    xsdryfcvbnmj    azxcsharpdsa

★ **Numerical adjectives**

Numerical adjectives show:

★ **number**

seven days; one hundred years; each child.

★ **the order of things**

first team; second week; final warning

★ **indefinite number**

some children; a few questions; several sweets

★ **Quantitative adjectives**

Quantitative adjectives show how much of something:
a little bit of luck; more cake; a whole bar of chocolate

**? Why use adjectives?**

Use adjectives to help make your writing more **interesting**.

**★ Other types of adjectives**

★ **Demonstrative adjectives** which point out things: this house; those children

★ **Possessive adjectives** show who or what owns them: my hand; their toys

★ **Interrogative adjectives** ask questions: Which house? Whose book?

**! Spotting adjectives**

★ An adjective is usually placed **immediately in front** of the word it describes: a *haunted* house

★ Many adjectives are linked to a noun by a verb: Dogs are *noisy*.

★ You can somtimes tell if a word is an adjective by the way it ends.

Here are some common adjective endings to remember:

**-able**: comfortable, reliable

**-y**: happy, sticky

**-al**: musical, vital

**-ary** : momentary, stationary

**-en**: broken, sunken

**-ful**: awful, helpful

**-ous**: serious, famous

**-ic**: poetic, terrific

**-ish**: childish, selfish

**-ive**: active, massive

## Similes

A simile helps us to describe things better. It compares two things. Similes often contain adjectives. Can you find all the adjectives in this simile poem?

> As wet as a fish – as dry as a bone;
> As live as a bird – as dead as a stone;
> As plump as a partridge – as poor as a rat;
> As strong as a horse – as weak as a cat;
> As hard as a flint – as soft as a mole;
> As white as a lily – as black as a coal.

## Comparison of adjectives

★ Comparative adjectives – When we compare two nouns we use comparative adjectives. These often end in er:
I am strong but Tom is stronger.

★ Superlative adjectives – These are used when we compare three or more things. They often end in est:
Sam is the strongest boy in my school.

## Try these . . .

Complete this chart. Take care with the spelling!

| root adjective | comparative adjective | superlative adjective |
|---|---|---|
| small | smaller | smallest |
| safe | | |
| hot | | |
| lucky | | |
| thin | | |
| hungry | | |

**Handy hint**

When we compare long adjectives it sounds silly if we add **er** or **est** to them:
beautifuller!
Use **more** or **most** in front of them:
beautiful – **more beautiful** – **most beautiful**.

**Irregular comparatives**

Some adjectives have irregular comparatives or superlatives:
good – better – best;
many – more – most;
little – less – least;
bad – worse – worst.

## Main features

**Main features of narrative texts**

★ re-tell imaginary events

★ contain dialogue (things people say)

★ usually written in the past tense

★ include a lot of descriptive language

★ usually written in the 3rd person.

## Narratives and recounts

At secondary school you will come across many different types of text. Understanding some of their features will help you deal with them more effectively.

### Narratives

The purpose of a narrative text is to entertain the reader.

### DIY survey

Carry out this survey on a story you are currently reading. Check out its features.

★ Select any passage from a story you are reading. Write down:

    a) the title of the story _____

    b) the author _____

    c) the page number of your chosen passage _____

★ Find and copy down ten verbs written in the past tense.

★ Find and write down some good examples of descriptive words used. (adjectives, adverbs, phrases etc.)

★ What person is the text written in – 1st, 2nd or 3rd person? _____ Find and write a sentence from the story as evidence to support your answer.

★ Find and write down different examples of 'dialogue' words used in the passage e.g. 'said', 'asked'.

## Recounts

We come across recounts every day in newspapers, on TV and at school. The purpose of a recount is to re-tell information or to give someone an account of events. A recount could be fictional (imaginary) or non-fiction (for information).

## Try this . . .

Read this recount about the life of William Shakespeare, the most famous writer in the world, and check out some of its features.

★ Give each paragraph a suitable heading.
★ Underline any verbs in the past tense. Are any of them action verbs?
★ Does it feature specific people and events?
★ Are the different events listed in order?

### Main features

★ Main features of recounts
  ★ to re-tell information or to give someone an account of events
  ★ often consist of a series of events organised in the order they happened
  ★ about specific events and people
  ★ written in the past tense
  ★ verbs are usually about actions

_____

William Shakespeare was born in Stratford in 1564, over four hundred years ago. He came from a wealthy family but when he was 15, William's father lost all his money. William was not able to stay on at school so he left and got a job. At 18 he met and fell in love with Anne Hathaway. They got married and soon started a family of their own.

_____

William decided to move to London and found work as an actor. He soon began writing his own plays. Queen Elizabeth loved music, poetry and plays. In fact she liked William's plays so much she asked him to write one especially for her. William always worked very hard. He and his friends built their own theatre, called 'The Globe', in London. William soon became rich and famous.

**⊘ Handy hint**

We often use full stops when words have been abbreviated: **p.m.**
But when the first and last letters of the word are included, we don't need a full stop: **Mrs**

**★ It's confusing, isn't it!**

If a questioning sentence is more of an exclamation than a question, use an exclamation mark:
**What do you think you look like!**

**★ Ellipsis . . .**

We sometimes use three dots at the end of a sentence if we wish to leave something to the reader's imagination:
**The door opened slowly . . .**

## Why bother with punctuation?

We use punctuation marks to make our writing easier to read and understand. Correct punctuation can make a lot of difference to the meaning!

Private. No swimming allowed.

Private? No! Swimming allowed.

Punctuation marks occur:

★ at the end of sentences

★ within sentences

## Punctuation marks at the end of sentences

**Full stop (.)** This is the most common punctuation mark at the end of a sentence.

**Question mark (?)** Do you know what a question mark is?

**Exclamation mark (!)** This is used to show someone feels strongly about something: How dare you!

## Punctuation within sentences

Comma (,) Commas are used to signal a pause to the reader. We use commas in different ways:

⭐ in lists: I like art, music, English and maths.

⭐ to separate bits added on to the beginning or ending of sentences: Joanne, pass me the newspaper, please.

⭐ to separate phrases or clauses: The car, an old wreck, was parked nearby.

| | |
|---|---|
| **Colon (:)** | A colon is used to show that an example, explanation or list is to follow: **You will need: 2 eggs, some flour, a pint of milk.** |
| **Semi-colon (;)** | A semi-colon is stronger than a comma but not as strong as a full stop. A semi-colon is often used to join two parts of a sentence without using a conjunction: **Tom jumped high; he headed in a great goal.** |
| **Dash (–)** | A dash holds words apart. It is stronger than a comma, but not as strong as a full stop: **I visited my favourite city – Paris.** |
| **Brackets ( )** | Brackets are used to enclose information to separate it from the rest of the sentence: **Paris (the capital of France) is a lovely city.** |

Top tip

ℹ️ Top tip
We don't need a comma after the word 'and' in a list.

✴️ Another use for semi-colons
We use semi-colons in long lists when the individual items in the list consist of more than one word.

Did you know...?

ℹ️ Dash it!
We sometimes use dashes to separate off words or phrases within a sentence: Roy Dougall — a brilliant footballer — plays for Blackburn Rovers.

# Silent letters

## History lesson

In earlier times the silent **k** in knife, **g** in gnaw and **w** in sword were all pronounced. They are really silent memorials to lost sounds!

## Blame it on the Romans!

Some words have Latin roots. For example, debt comes from the Latin debitum, and receipt from receptum, which explains where the silent **b** and **p** come from in each word.

## What are silent letters?

Some words are difficult to spell because they contain silent letters (letters we don't pronounce when we say the words), such as **k**nit, **w**rist, num**b**. There are often interesting historical reasons for silent letters.

## Try it yourself ▼

We can work out rules about when silent letters occur. Fill in the missing silent **g**, **k** or **w** in each word. Use a dictionary if necessary.

| | | | |
|---|---|---|---|
| **k** nowledge | ___nu | ___reck | ___narled |
| ___not | ___rite | ___nome | ___neel |
| ___rap | ___rong | ___nit | ___ren |
| ___nash | ___riggle | ___nat | ___nuckle |
| ___naw | ___rinkle | ___night | ___retch |

### Now work out and complete the rule for each silent letter.

| Rule 1 | When a silent **g** comes at the beginning of a word it is always followed by the letter ___. |
|---|---|
| Rule 2 | When a silent **k** comes at the beginning of a word it is always followed by the letter ___. |
| Rule 3 | When a silent **w** comes at the beginning of a word it is always followed by the letter ___. |

## Summary of helpful rules

Complete the table below. Add another example for each rule. Use a dictionary if necessary.

| silent letter | rule | examples |
|---|---|---|
| b | often preceded by m at the end of words | **tom**b |
| b | sometimes followed by t | subtle |
| c | often preceded by s | scent |
| e | often preceded by a consonant at the end of a word | game |
| g | often followed by n | gnome |
| h | sometimes preceded by g or r | ghost<br>rhubarb |
| h | sometimes comes at the beginning of a word and is followed by o | hour |
| k | often followed by n | knit |
| l | often followed by k or m | yolk<br>palm |
| n | usually preceded by m | column |
| p | often followed by n or s | pneumonia<br>psalm |
| s | sometimes followed by l | aisle |
| t | often preceded by s | bristle |
| u | may sometimes follow c or g | biscuit<br>guitar |

**? Love or lov?**

The explanation of the silent e at the end of words like love, give, have, above, live goes back to a time when u and v were written in the same way. To indicate that the consonant v was intended (and not the vowel u) a silent e was added to the end!

**! What a difference an e can make!**

In many words the final e is not pronounced, like made, theme, hope, cute, wine – but if we leave it off, see what happens!

**★ Take it easy**

We tend to pronounce words the easiest way, so today we tend to find it easier to leave out sounds (like r in February and d in handsome), which then become silent letters.

# Parts of speech — Adverbs

All the words in our language may be divided into groups, known as 'parts of speech' (or 'word classes'). Each part of speech has a particular job to do in a sentence.

## Adverbs

An adverb tells us more about a verb. It adds meaning to the verb.
Usually adverbs come as close as possible to the verbs they describe:
The boy shouted loudly.

## Types of adverb

### Adverbs of manner

These answer the question 'How?': The cow mooed softly.
Many adverbs of manner may be formed by adding the suffix ly to adjectives.
Sometimes the spelling of the root adjective remains unchanged:
loud – loudly.
Sometimes the spelling of the root adjective is changed:
hungry – hungrily.

## Try these . . .

1. Find the adjective
   in each group of letters.

   Change each adjective
   into an adverb of manner.

   **abcdhumble** _____

   **bnoisyzxcvbn** _____

   **zxtruthfulcv** _____

2. Replace the underlined words with an adverb of manner ending in ly.
   a) The singer left the stage <u>in a hurry</u>. (_____)
   b) I answered all the questions <u>with ease</u>. (_____)
   c) The baby was sleeping <u>in peace</u>. (_____)

---

**? Why use adverbs?**
Use adverbs to help make your writing more interesting.

**★ Spotting adverbs**
Usually an adverb goes as close as possible to the verb it is describing. Many adverbs end in **ly**.

**! Handy hint**
Use the phrase 'in a ... way' instead of an adverb from time to time. Sometimes it is much easier and sounds better:
Tom behaved in a polite way.

★ **Adverbs of place**

These answer the question 'Where?':

The dog wanted to go <u>outside</u>.

★ **Adverbs of time**

These answer the question 'When?':

My uncle arrived <u>late</u>.

★ **Adverbs of reason**

These answer the question 'Why?':

The game was cancelled <u>because</u> of the fog.

★ **Adverbs of number**

These answer the question 'How many?':

He did the same thing <u>twice</u>.

★ **Adverbs of degree**

These answer the questions 'How much?' or 'To what extent?':

Tom was <u>very</u> upset.

## Comparison of adverbs

**Comparative adverbs** – When we compare two situations we use comparative adverbs:

The male lion came <u>nearer</u> than the female.

**Superlative adverbs** – These are used when we compare three or more situations:

Of all the children, Sam arrived <u>earliest</u>.

The usual ways of showing the comparative and superlative are:

★ by adding **er** and **est** if the adverb has only one syllable: soon – sooner – soonest

★ by placing **more** or **most** in front of the adverb if it has more than one syllable: sincerely – more sincerely – most sincerely

**Take care!**

★ Just because a word ends in **ly** doesn't mean it is an adverb! Here are some examples: **fly, bully, ugly, holy**

★ Some adverbs have their own special forms: **soon, now, here, also**

★ Some adverbs are the same as their adjectives: **fast, long, near, close**

★ Don't use an adjective when you need an adverb:

He writes much neater. (wrong)

He writes much more neatly. (correct)

Why doesn't she speak proper? (wrong)

Why doesn't she speak properly? (correct)

# Parts of speech – Conjunctions

**★ Connectives**

Conjunctions are sometimes also called connectives.

**⚠ Beware!**

Sometimes conjunctions may consist of more than one word: **We played the game even though it was raining.**

Here are a few examples: **even though; as far as; so that; in order that; now that; even if; as long as**

**⚠ Handy hint**

There are two clues in the word 'conjunction' to help you remember what it is. Clue 1. The prefix 'con' is Latin and means to compound (or join together). Clue 2. A road 'junction' is where two or more roads come together.

All the words in our language may be divided into groups, known as 'parts of speech' (or 'word classes'). Each part of speech has a particular job to do in a sentence.

## What is a conjunction?

A conjunction is a joining word. Conjunctions are words that connect parts of a sentence. We often use a conjunction to join two short sentences together to make one longer sentence.

I put up my umbrella. It was raining. (two sentences)
I put up my umbrella because it was raining. (one sentence with a conjunction)

## Common conjunctions

Some common conjunctions are:

| and | because | but | for | however | since | until | yet |

Choose the best conjunction to join these ideas together to make one sentence.

1. It was very hot _____ (since/so) it was a relief to get into the shade.
2. I will not speak to Julia _____ (because/unless) she does not like me.
3. I went to bed _____ (so that/as) I could get some sleep.
4. I try to do my homework _____ (although/before) I watch TV.
5. I didn't stop trying _____ (until/during) the game had finished.

36

# Types of conjunction

There are four types of conjunction, depending on the job they do in the sentence. These are:

★ co-ordinating ★ contrasting ★ co-relative ★ subordinating

### ★ Co-ordinating conjunctions

Co-ordinating conjunctions are used when the things joined are basically similar and complement each other.

Common co-ordinating conjunctions are: and, as

I sat down and ate my tea.

Tom went shopping, as did Sam.

### ★ Contrasting conjunctions

Contrasting conjunctions are used when the things joined are basically different.

Common contrasting conjunctions are: but, however, yet

I am good at art but Ben is good at spelling.

### ★ Co-relative conjunctions

Co-relative conjunctions are used to show that the two things joined are similar.

Common co-relative conjunctions are: both + and; either + or; so + as; not only + but also

You can drive either the silver car or the red one.

### ★ Subordinating conjunctions

Subordinating conjunctions are used when one thing depends on another.

Common subordinating conjunctions are: after, because, for, since, until, when, although

I stayed indoors until it stopped raining.

# Varying your style

Sometimes you can make things sound a little more interesting by beginning a sentence with a conjunction.

You won't get any pocket money unless you tidy your room. (conjunction in the middle)

Unless you tidy your room, you won't get any pocket money. (conjunction at the beginning)

---

**Don't worry!**

Don't worry too much about the names of the different types of conjunction. Think more about the sort of job each type of conjunction does!

**? Did you know . . .?**

We only ever begin a sentence with 'and' or 'but' if we wish to emphasise a point:

He fell off his bike. He got a puncture. But Jack did not get upset.

**Try it yourself**

Rewrite each sentence and begin it with the conjunction.

1. Mrs Barnes took off her coat after she got home.
2. Mr Green watched television while he ate his tea.
3. I visit my uncle whenever I have time.
4. You can't go out as you have been misbehaving.

# Sentences and clauses

## Phrases

A **phrase** is a group of words that do not make sense on their own. Most phrases are short. Most phrases do not contain verbs.

The girls ran <u>along the beach</u> (along the beach is a phrase)

## Simple sentences

A **simple** sentence is made up of **one** clause.

Each simple sentence has **two** parts:

★ a subject (who or what the sentence is about)

★ a predicate (the rest of the sentence, including the verb)

<u>The evil-looking pirate</u> (subject) <u>waved his sword</u>. (predicate – the verb is <u>waved</u>.)

## What is a clause?

A clause is a group of words that may be used as a whole sentence, or as part of a sentence. A clause must contain a subject and a verb.

This is a simple one-clause sentence:
The prince (subject) smiled (verb).

## Simple one-clause sentences

Check that there is only one clause in each sentence below.
Underline the subject and circle the verb in each of these simple sentences.
1. The pop singer played a guitar.
2. The angry dog barked loudly.
3. The sheep grazed on the hillside.
4. My favourite football team won the cup.
5. Submarines travel underwater.

## Two-clause sentences

Some sentences have more than one clause:
I picked the flowers (clause 1) which grew in my garden. (clause 2)

## Single or double? Check it out!

Look for the verbs in these sentences.
Does each sentence consist of one or two clauses?
The submarine <u>sank</u> slowly to the ocean floor. (<u>one</u>)
The clouds parted and the moon shone through. (____)
The film began dramatically. (____)
Elephants trumpet but lions growl. (____)
I ran to the shop before it closed. (____)
The old lady with the funny hat drove dangerously. (____)

**The first is done for you**

## Complex sentences

A complex sentence contains one main clause and one or more subordinate (less important) clause. A subordinate clause does not make sense on its own:
I will come (main clause) as soon as I can. (subordinate clause)

## Try this . . .

Choose the best way of joining the main clause and subordinate clause together in these complex sentences.

I ran away from the bull _____ (after/which) was chasing me.

The cat chased the bird _____ (when/since) it landed on the grass.

I know the lady _____ (who/which) lives in that big house.

The children ran to school _____ (in case/in order that) they were late.

**Did you know...?**

Beware!
Sometimes the main clause in a sentence is split, with the subordinate clause in the middle:
That boy over there (1st part of main clause)
who has the punk haircut (subordinate clause)
is my brother (2nd part of main clause)

39

## Features of instructional texts

★ information written in a clear and ordered way, to make it easy to follow

★ contain lots of specific information, for example on how to do something

★ often have lots of 'time' words to link instructions, e.g. 'first'

★ verbs are in the present tense

★ verbs are often in the imperative form, e.g. 'Turn to page 10'

★ verbs are written in the 2nd person, although the pronoun 'you' is often missed out, for example '(You) Peel the bananas'

## Instructional texts and information reports

At secondary school you will come across many different types of text. Understanding some of their features will help you deal with them more effectively.

## Instructional texts

The purpose of an instructional text is to tell someone how to do something or to give directions. We come across instructions or directions on bottles, boxes, in books at school and so on.

## Try this . . .

★ Read the text below telling you how to make a banana milkshake. Follow the instructions and check out the features of the text!

★ Number the instructions in the 'What you do' section in the correct order.

★ Underline and 'time' words you can find in the instructions, which tell you when to do things.

★ Circle the imperative verbs in each instruction. Are they in the present tense?

## What you need
★ 2 cups of cold milk      ★ 2 medium bananas
★ 4 scoops of ice cream      ★ some 'sprinkles' for decoration

## What you do
____ After this, add the ice cream and mix it in.
____ Enjoy your milkshakes with a friend!
____ Lastly, put some 'sprinkles' on top to make it look nice.
____ Then mash them with a fork.
____ Next add the milk and stir until the mixture is smooth.
____ Firstly peel the bananas
____ Following this, serve up your milkshakes in glasses.

# Information reports

The purpose of an information report is to present information in a straightforward factual manner. Much of the studying you do at secondary school involves reading non-fiction books containing information.

## Try it yourself ▼

**Read this information recount and check it out.**

★ Does it contain lots of facts?
★ Is it about one particular elephant or about elephants in general?
★ Is the language quite formal, or chatty and friendly?
★ Is it written in the present or past tense?
★ Is it written in the 1st, 2nd or 3rd person?

The elephant is the largest living land animal. There are two kinds of elephant. The Indian elephant can be trained to work. The larger African elephant is not easily trained. A big male, or bull, may weigh seven tonnes. Elephants live in herds. If one elephant is injured, the rest will help it. Elephants eat huge amounts of grass and tree leaves every day.

## Did you know...?

★ **Features of information reports**

★ contain many facts
★ language used is factual and precise, rather than imaginative
★ language is usually quite formal
★ subject of the report normally a whole group of things, for example 'pandas' rather than one specific panda
★ often written in the present tense
★ usually written in the 3rd person

# Punctuating speech

## Why do we use speech marks?

We use speech marks (' ' or " ") to signal the beginning and end of words used by a speaker when we write them down.

## Direct speech

When we write down the actual words used by a speaker we call this direct speech.

## Rules for punctuating direct speech

| | |
|---|---|
| Rule 1 | Only the words that are actually spoken should go inside the speech marks: Mrs Smith said, "I am going shopping." |
| Rule 2 | Begin the first word the person says inside speech marks with a capital letter, as it is really the beginning of a sentence: The teacher shouted, 'Stop running!' |
| Rule 3 | Always use a comma before opening speech marks: Mrs Jones said, 'Hello.' |
| Rule 4 | Always use some form of punctuation mark before closing speech marks: 'It's four o'clock,' Tom said. |
| Rule 5 | When a quotation is interrupted in mid-sentence, you do not need a capital letter when you re-open the speech marks again: 'It's so cold,' muttered Anna, 'my teeth are chattering.' |
| Rule 6 | Always start a new line whenever a different person begins to speak: 'Where are you going with that ball?' my mum asked. 'I'm going into the garden,' I replied. |

# So – what have you learned?

Rewrite the following passage in direct speech in the blank space below. Punctuate the sentences correctly.

Where are you going with that ball my mum asked I'm going into the garden I replied What are you going to do she asked I'm going to practise heading the ball against the wall I answered But the garden's too small my mum exclaimed Don't worry I'll be careful I assured her Make sure you don't head the ball near the windows my mother warned I won't I replied with a grin

## Vary your sentence structures

It makes your writing more interesting if you vary the way you write down direct speech: Ali said, "I can stand on my head." or "I can stand on my head," Ali said.

## Reported (or indirect) speech

In reported speech you report what has been said but you don't quote it word for word. Note the difference between reported and direct speech:

"I like sweets," the girl said (direct speech)

The girl said that she liked sweets (reported speech)

## Overused words

The word 'said' is one of the most overused words in our language. Use a thesaurus to help you find more interesting ways of expressing the word.

# Tricky spellings

## Unstressed vowels

We don't always say every sound in every word. This can lead to spelling mistakes. Some words with more than one syllable contain unstressed vowels that are hard to hear, for example interest. Use a dictionary to help you spell words containing unstressed vowels.

## Double trouble

Double letters in words can cause trouble.

**Rule** In words with one syllable containing a short vowel in the middle, we must double the final consonant before adding a suffix beginning with a vowel: stop – stopping, stopped, stopper

## Try this . . .

Make some new words by suffixing all of the words you can. (NB You won't be able to suffix every word!)

| root word | + suffix er | + suffix est | + suffix ing | + suffix ed |
|---|---|---|---|---|
| hop | hopper | | hopping | hopped |
| fit | | | | |
| hot | | | | |
| flat | | | | |
| plan | | | | |
| jog | | | | |
| big | | | | |
| ban | | | | |

## Mnemonics

Mnemonics are memory aids to help you remember the spelling of tricky words. Making up a silly sentence involving some key feature of a word is one form of mnemonic. For example:

There is a rat in separate!

## DIY mnemonics

Make up some mnemonics of your own.

Choose a word from the box to complete each mnemonic.

| | | | |
|---|---|---|---|
| young | bicycle | piece | busy |
| friend | build | believe | great |

1. The bus was _____.
2. Never _____ a lie.
3. I would like a _____ of pie.
4. You are only _____ once.
5. I will be your _____ till the very end.
6. It's _____ to eat.
7. U and i can _____ a wall.
8. Don't ride a _____ in icy weather.

### ★ More mnemonics

Some good mnemonics to remember are:

★ What's the weight of eight people?

★ A miser is always miserable.

★ There's a cog in recognise.

★ The captain is the main officer.

★ I am a bit ambitious.

★ Conscience has science in it.

★ There are three e's buried in a cemetery.

★ My secretary can keep a secret.

# Word-building with affixes

**Did you know...?**

## ★ Affixes

An **affix** is the bit of a word that can be added to the **beginning** or **end** of a word to make a longer word. There are two sorts of affix:

- ★ prefixes (like un- as in unhappy)
- ★ suffixes (like -ing as in laughing)

## ! Prefixes and spelling

If you understand this simple rule, you will avoid lots of silly spelling mistakes:

When you add a prefix to a root word, the spelling of the root word remains unchanged:

**dis + appear = disappear**.

## Root words

A root word is a basic word to which a prefix and/or a suffix may be added to make a different word:

- ★ help (root word)
- ★ help**ful** (root word + suffix)
- ★ **un**help**ful** (root word + suffix and prefix)

## Try this . . .

These words have all had affixes added. Underline the root word in each case. The first one has been done for you.

| | | | |
|---|---|---|---|
| bi<u>cycle</u> | triangle | exported | injustice |
| friendliness | uncontrollable | magician | disagreement |
| clearly | signature | unsuitable | freedom |

## Prefixes

A prefix is a group of letters that is added to the beginning of a word. Prefixes often have a particular meaning:
bi means 'two' so bisect means 'to cut in two'.
Try to learn as many prefix meanings as possible. This will help you guess the meanings of lots of words you didn't know before.

## Try these . . .

Add the prefix to each word. Look up its meaning in a dictionary. Can you find any other words beginning with the same prefix?

a) auto + mobile   b) bi + lingual   c) dis + agree   d) extra + ordinary

e) il + legal   f) inter + view   g) micro + scope   h) aqua + plane

## Suffixes

A suffix is a group of letters that is added to the end of a root word.

A suffix may change the meaning of the word: care – caring

A suffix may change the job the word does: good (adjective) – goodness (noun).

## Try these ...

Underline the suffix in each word. Then write the root word to which the suffix has been added. The first one has been done for you. Take care! The spelling of the root word will need altering a little each time.

beautiful – beauty

awful – _____

Portuguese – _____

wondrous – _____

ignorant – _____

argument – _____

roguish – _____

responsible – _____

wisdom – _____

happiness – _____

cyclist – _____

communication – _____

### ★ Prefixes and their meanings

Here are a few common prefixes and their meanings:

| prefix | meaning | example |
|--------|---------|---------|
| pre | before | prefix |
| anti | against | antiseptic |
| mis | wrong | misspell |
| multi | many | multi-storey |
| semi | half | semicircle |
| ex | out of | export |

### ★ Common suffixes

**Nouns:**

-er (boxer);

-tion (revolution);

-ance (appearance);

-ment (advertisement);

-ery (discovery);

-ure (exposure)

**Verbs:**

-en (frighten);

-fy (horrify);

-ing (making);

-ed (talked)

**Adjectives:**

-al (musical);

-ic (angelic);

-ful (careful);

-less (hopeless);

-ous (dangerous);

-able (comfortable)

**Adverbs:**

-ly (clearly)

# Punctuation in words

## Note this

Hyphens are also used:

★ to separate some prefixes from their root words: co-ordinate, pre-eminent

★ to avoid confusion with similar words: re-cover or recover?

★ when coupled with capital letters: U-turn

NB If you are unsure, always use a dictionary to check.

## Take care!

A common mistake is to confuse the possessive pronoun **its** (The monster opened its mouth ) with the contraction **it's**, meaning 'it is' (It's too hot to go out.).

**Take care!**

## Why bother with punctuation?

We use punctuation marks to make our writing easier to read and understand. Correct punctuation can make a lot of difference to the meaning!

★ The king walked into the room half an hour after he was beheaded!

★ The king walked into the room. Half an hour after, he was beheaded.

## Hyphens

Hyphens keep words together to help make their meaning clear. They are used to join two or more words to make compound words:
I love freshly-baked bread.

## Try it yourself ▼

### Join each pair of these words with a hyphen.

Use each compound word correctly in the sentences below.

clean shaven     hard working     passer by     long necked

Kate always did all her homework. She was very

_____.

The thief did not have a beard. He was _____.

A giraffe is a _____ animal.

The _____ stopped to look in the window.

## Apostrophes in contractions

We sometimes shorten words by missing out some letters. We call these words contractions. We use an apostrophe (') to show where there are letters missing: can't = can not.

# Apostrophes to show ownership

We use an apostrophe to show ownership (to show that something belongs to someone). Follow some simple rules and it's easy!

**Rule 1** When the owner is singular, we usually write 's after the noun:
the clown's hat = the hat belonging to the clown.

## Try this . . .

Write the missing short forms, using an apostrophe correctly.

| short form with apostrophe | longer form |
| --- | --- |
| the king's robe | the robe belonging to the king |
| | the card belonging to Ben |
| | the hat belonging to the lady |
| | the cow belonging to the farmer |
| | the case belonging to Mr Shah |

## Try this . . .

**Rule 2** Many plural nouns end in s. To show ownership we put the apostrophe after the s: the girls' bags = the bags belonging to the girls.

**Rule 3** When a plural noun does not end with s, we show ownership by adding 's: the men's car = the car belonging to the men.

Write the missing short forms, using an apostrophe correctly.

| short form with apostrophe | longer form |
| --- | --- |
| | the nest belonging to the ants |
| | the car park belonging to the teachers |
| | the book belonging to the children |
| | the antlers belonging to the deer |

## Mistakes all around!

Many adults don't fully understand the correct use of apostrophes. You will often find mistakes all around you (in shop signs, magazines etc.).

**Sallys café**
*Todays special – sausage's and chip's*

## Some more apostrophe rules

★ Where adding 's to a noun produces an ugly or difficult sound, drop the s: Jesus' disciples

★ Use an apostrophe to show an amount of time: a week's time

★ Use apostrophes to form plurals of letters that don't normally have plurals: p's and q's

**49**

# Parts of speech — Prepositions

All the words in our language may be divided into groups, known as 'parts of speech' (or 'word classes'). Each part of speech has a particular job to do in a sentence.

## What is a preposition?

A preposition is a word that links two nouns (or pronouns):

The train went through the tunnel.

(The preposition 'through' shows how 'train' and 'tunnel' are linked.)

Carl was a member of the football team.

(The preposition 'of' shows how 'Carl' and 'football team' are linked.)

## Common prepositions

Here is a word wall of common prepositions.

| about | above | across | after | against | along |
|---|---|---|---|---|---|
| | amid | around | at | before | behind |
| below | beneath | beside | between | beyond | by |
| | down | except | for | from | inside |
| in | like | near | of | off | over |
| | since | through | till | to | towards |
| under | until | up | upon | with | |

### Handy hint

Prepositions often tell us about position:

The apple was in the bag.

The prefix 'pre' is Latin for 'in front of' so the name 'preposition' suggests a position in a sentence in front of something.

### Spotting prepositions

To spot a preposition, look for more than one noun or pronoun in a sentence, then check to see if they are linked in some way. Look for the word that shows how they are linked. This will be the preposition: The mouse was under the chair.

50

## Try these . . .

1. Find the ten propositions hidden in this puzzle.

```
q   w   u   p   x   a   r   d   r   e
t   y   p   z   d   o   w   n   a   s
a   o   f   f   d   f   g   h   j   k
l   m   n   b   v   x   o   v   e   r
z   v   u   n   d   e   r   h   g   t
w   t   q   r   o   u   n   d   f   g
h   b   v   b   e   t   w   e   e   n
u   p   o   n   b   h   y   r   w   d
q   w   a   b   o   v   e   k   l   j
m   n   v   b   e   l   o   w   x   z
```

**Compound prepositions**

Compound prepositions consist of more than one word, like these:

apart from;

because of;

in front of.

BEWARE!

2. Think of a suitable preposition to go where one is missing.

a) The child hid _____ the bed.

b) You get _____ of a car.

c) The horse galloped _____ the field.

d) You dive _____ a swimming pool.

e) The child stood _____ his parents.

**Beware!**

Some words may be used as both prepositions and adverbs.

The farmer put a fence round his field.

(preposition – because it links two nouns)

The farmer turned round.

(adverb)

# Spelling rules

## Why bother with spelling rules?

It is helpful to learn and remember some spelling rules, and follow them to help you spell well.

**Rule 1** Remember to put i (when it sounds like ee) before e except after c:

believe (i before e) but receive (not after c).

### Try this . . .

Follow the rule above. Mark these spellings. There are seven mistakes.

1. shriek ❑
2. recieve ❑
3. priest ❑
4. ceiling ❑
5. mischeif ❑
6. piece ❑
7. decieve ❑
8. shield ❑
9. releif ❑
10. conceit ❑
11. yeild ❑
12. believe ❑
13. reciept ❑
14. greif ❑
15. perceive ❑

**Rule 2** When a word ends with a consonant + y, change the y to i before adding a suffix:

baby – babies; lazy – lazily

---

**Follow the rules but . . .**
Rules are very helpful – but there are always words that don't stick to them. Here are some exceptions to Rule 1: science, quiet, weird, caffeine, protein, seize

**Why oh, why?**
When adding y to a word ending in e, drop the before adding the y:
ease – easy;
ice – icy;
stone – stony;
noise – noisy etc.

## Try this . . .

⭐ **Write the plural of each noun:**
a) baby – babies    b) lorry _____    c) supply _____

⭐ **Add <u>ness</u> to each adjective to change it into a noun:**
a) happy – happiness    b) lazy _____    c) pretty _____

⭐ **Add <u>ous</u> to each noun to change it into an adjective:**
a) glory – glorious    b) fury _____    c) mystery _____

⭐ **Change each adjective into an adverb by adding <u>ly</u>:**
a) tidy – tidily    b) weary _____    c) hungry _____

⭐ **Write the comparative and superlative forms of these adjectives:**
a) lucky – luckier – luckiest    b) noisy _____
c) heavy _____    d) busy _____

⭐ **Complete these verbs:**
a) marry – marries – married    b) hurry _____
c) rely _____    d) multiply _____

## DIY rules

It is a good idea to look for patterns in spelling and try to work out rules to help you. Look at each set of example words then work out the rule.

Set 1 protect – protection; collect – collection;
     direct – direction

> Rule: To change verbs ending in ct into nouns we just add _____.

Set 2 generate – generation; hibernate – hibernation;
     evacuate – evacuation

> Rule: To change verbs ending in ate into nouns we
> _____.

Look for patterns

⭐ **Keep the e (1)**
When you add a suffix beginning with a consonant to a word ending in a silent e, always retain the silent e:
hope – hopeful;
brave – bravely;
late – lateness.

⭐ **Keep the e (2)**
When you add a suffix beginning with a or o after a soft c or g, always retain the silent e to keep the c or g 'soft':
notice – noticeable;
outrage – outrageous.

# Types of text

At secondary school you will come across many different types of text. Understanding some of their features will help you deal with them more effectively.

## Explanatory texts

In schools we come across many explanations in books. The purpose of an explanatory text is to give an explanation of how something works or to answer questions about something.

## Try this . . .

Look at this diagram explaining how the water cycle works. Check out the features of the text.

★ What process is being explained?

★ Is the explanation given clearly in a step by step way?

★ Does the diagram help the explanation? How?

★ Are the verbs in the present or past tense?

★ Can you find any examples of passive verbs in the explanation?

### Features of explanatory texts

★ explain a process or how something works

★ often incorporate diagrams or pictures

★ use step by step approach, each step clearly explained

★ often use present tense verbs

★ often use passive verbs, e.g. The buzzer is connected to a battery.

The water vapour turns into small drops of water. Clouds are formed from these drops of water.

As the clouds pass over high mountains and hills, water is dropped in the form of rain or snow.

Water is warmed by the sun. It turns into water vapour and rises.

The water is carried down and back towards the sea by streams and rivers.

54

# Discursive texts

In school we are often asked to discuss things. It is important to look at things from different perspectives. The purpose of a discursive text is to present a balanced argument to your reader.

## Try this . . .

Read what the main features of a discursive text are. Use the outline below to help you write an argument for and against shortening the school day.

I think shortening the school day is a _____ idea.

I have several reasons to support this.

My first reason is _____.

My second reason is _____.

My third reason is _____.

Some people do not agree.

Here are some of their reasons.

_____

_____

What do you think?

## Features of discursive texts

★ attempt to present a balanced argument

★ make clear writer's point of view

★ also present other possible points of view

★ contain arguments in favour of and against an issue

★ encourage the reader to make up their own mind

★ often contain persuasive language

★ often contain conditional verbs such as 'should' and 'must'

# The history of our language

The English language changes all the time. If we travelled back in time to the Norman period, we would not be able to understand much of what people said. Our language is not just one language. The words in our language come from different people and places that have had contact with Great Britain in the past.

## Borrowed words

Over the years we have borrowed many words from other languages.

## Try this . . .

All the following words have been borrowed from other languages. Can you guess where they originally came from? Use a dictionary to help you.

wok (China)       boomerang (_____)       café (_____)

bungalow (_____)    yacht (_____)    moccasin (_____)

reggae (_____)    hamburger (_____)    banana (_____)

chocolate (_____)      mosque (_____)      sauna (_____)

## Our Roman roots

We owe many root words to our Roman past.

### Try it yourself ▼

Match up each English word below to the Latin root word that it comes from.

**English words**

anniversary    temporary    dental    amiable
movement    proverb    abbreviate    manufacture

**Latin root words**

amo (meaning: I love)    dentis (meaning: tooth)    manus (meaning: hand)
moveo (meaning: I move)    verbum (meaning: word)    tempus (meaning: time)
annus (meaning: year)    brevis (meaning: short)

---

### ★ Use a dictionary

Some dictionaries tell you where words came from (their etymology). Look at this example:

cotton (n) [from Arabic *qutun*] soft white seed hairs of various plants from which material can be made.

### ? The Italian connection

Many of our words come from Italy. Lots of them end with the vowels a, i and o.

How many of these Italian words are to do with music or food?

| | |
|---|---|
| pizza | opera |
| solo | pasta |
| spaghetti | confetti |
| cello | studio |
| ravioli | macaroni |
| umbrella | volcano |

# The origins of place names

Many place names have interesting origins: Birmingham originally meant the people (ing) of the village (ham) of Birm. The Anglo-Saxons named many places in Britain.

## Try this . . .

Here are some Anglo-Saxon words and their meanings. Use an atlas. Find some British place names containing these Anglo-Saxon words.

| ing | people of that place | minster | a church |
|-----|----------------------|---------|----------|
| ton (or tun) | a farm | chester | a place with a Roman fort |
| ford | a place to cross a river | bourne | a stream or boundary |
| wick (or wich) | a group of houses | lea (or leigh) | an open space in a wood |

## Words take on new meanings

Our language is a living thing. Many words and expressions may change their meanings over time. For example, a mouse can be an animal that squeaks – but now it can also be something to move a cursor around a computer screen!

## Try these . . .

Here are the original meanings of some words. Can you think of a more recent meaning for them?
keen (sharp); flat (level); hack (to chop); trainer (someone who trains others); web (something spiders spin); film (a thin covering); pop (a loud noise); awful (full of awe and wonder); terrific (causing terror); nice (fussy); naughty (worth nothing)

**It's all Greek to me!**
Many prefixes have Greek origins:
**auto** means **self** as in **autobiography**;
**dia** means **through** as in **diameter**;
**syl** means **together** as in **syllable**;
**tele** means **from afar** as in **telephone**;
**octo** means **eight** as in **octopus**;
**micro** means **small** as in **microscope**

## Inventing new words
We have to continually invent new words to describe new things. All these words have recently entered our language. Can you think of any more?
wheelie; countdown; aerosol; supersonic; newscaster; supermarket; astronaut

# Glossary of useful English terms

**Adjective**
An adjective is a describing word. It gives more meaning to a noun: A fierce lion
When we compare nouns we use comparative or superlative adjectives:
fat – fatter – fattest

**Adverb**
An adverb is a word that gives more meaning to a verb. They often end in ly:
The girl ran quickly.

**Antonyms**
Antonyms are words whose meanings are as different as possible from each other:
big/small

**Clause**
A clause is a group of words that can be used either as a whole sentence or as part of a sentence. A clause always contains a verb.

**Conjunction**
A conjunction is a joining word.
Conjunctions are often used to join two sentences together:
I went home and I watched television.

**Direct speech**
Direct speech refers to the words actually spoken in a conversation. These words go inside speech marks.

**Homophone**
Homophones are words that sound the same but have a different meaning:
I have a pain in my stomach. I broke the pane of glass.

**Indirect Speech**
Indirect speech is also sometimes called reported speech. The exact words a person says are not used. Speech marks are not used: For example: The lady said that the shop was closed.

**Noun**
A noun is a naming word. It can be the name of a person, place or thing. Ordinary nouns are called common nouns:
a boy, a river, a pencil
A proper noun is the particular name of a person, place or thing.
It always begins with a capital letter: The man's name was Sam. He lived in Kingston.
A collective noun is the name of a group of something: a flock of sheep
An abstract noun is the name of a feeling or idea: love, jealousy, anger
Nouns may be singular (meaning one: a car) or plural (meaning more than one: lots of cars).
Nouns may have a different gender. This refers to the sex of the object. A word may be masculine: man; feminine: girl; common: child; neuter: table.

**Object**
Some sentences have a subject and an object:
The girl threw the ball.

**Paragraph**
A paragraph is a group of sentences that deals with one main idea or topic.

**Preposition**
A preposition tells us the position of one thing in relation to another. For example, The cat is on the mat.

**Prefix**
A prefix is a group of letters we add to the beginning of a word to change its meaning: happy – unhappy

**Pronoun**
A pronoun is a word we use in place of a noun.

**Punctuation**
Punctuation helps us make sense of what we read. Punctuation marks make writing easier for us to understand.

| | |
|---|---|
| Simile | A simile is when we liken one thing to another:<br>The baby's skin was as smooth as silk. |
| Subject | The subject of a sentence is the person or thing the sentence is all about:<br>The man ran fast. |
| Suffix | A suffix is a group of letters we add to the end of a word to change its meaning:<br>spider/spiders; cook/cooking |
| Syllable | Longer words may be broken into smaller parts called syllables.<br>cat has one syllable; cat/ching has two syllables |
| Synonym | Synonyms are words with the same, or similar, meanings: A sad, unhappy child |
| Verb | A verb is a doing or being word:<br>The lion was huge. It roared loudly.<br>An auxiliary verb is a small 'helper' verb:<br>The children are shouting.<br>Verbs may be written in different tenses. The tense of a verb changes according to the time of the action. For example:<br>Now I am riding a bicycle. (present tense)<br>Yesterday I rode a bicycle. (past tense)<br>Tomorrow I will ride a bicycle. (future tense) |

# Answers

## Looking carefully at words

*Try this...*
watch, match, fetch, sketchbook, stitch, patch,
scratches, itches, ketchup, kitchen, hutch,
latch, catch, switch.

*Try these....*
bare, dare, rare, scare, stare, glare, beware, prepare
were, mere, where, there
hire, wire, tire, dire, mire, spire, shire, require
bore, core, wore, tore, score, store, snore, before
cure, sure, lure, injure, secure, measure, pleasure, treasure

*Pattern puzzler*
tough, though, cough
learn, search, early
hedge, badge, smudge
furniture, fracture, creature
nation, education, instruction
fourteen, journey, humour

*Try it yourself*
ai   (said)
arm  (swarm)
all  (shall)
ine  (machine)
ive  (expensive)
oes  (shoes)

*Take a word!*
fed
sting
sing
mess
price

*Enough's enough*
6 different ways

## Parts of speech – nouns

*Common nouns*
teacher, dentist, nurse, artist
harbour, garage, hangar, bank
apple, bike, mug, ruler

*Proper nouns*
1. Tom and Sam went to the Ritz cinema in Milton Keynes.
2. Yesterday was Wednesday, the last day of March.
3. Roald Dahl wrote James and the Giant Peach.

*Abstract nouns*
danger
honesty
patience

*Collective nouns*
1. a collection of stamps     a bunch of bananas
2. a herd of elephants        a flock of sheep
3. a pile of stones           a swarm of bees

## Using a dictionary

*Try this...*
a) rearm, recall, redirect, report
b) postcode, postdate, postgraduate, postpone
c) superfine, supernatural, supersonic, supervise

*Try it yourself*
professor
necessary
disappear
recommend
harass
succeed
marvellous
possession

## More about nouns

*Animals*
cow      bull
gander   goose
mare     stallion
hind     hart
ewe      ram

*Try this...*
Masculine   duke, wizard, bachelor
Feminine    nun, grandmother, bride
Common      pupil, doctor, friend
Neuter      tap, hotel, box

## Counting syllables

*Try this...*
Two syllables   insult, careless, district, tennis, transport, exclude,
                helpful
Three syllables conductor, hospital, furniture, suspension,
                finishing, universe

Four syllables    photography, information, thermometer, machinery, astonishment

*Syllable sums*
impolitely, explanation, remembering, preparation, procession, (could also be concession or recession), illogical, enlighten, considering

## Parts of speech – verbs

*Regular verbs*

| | |
|---|---|
| I jumped | I will jump |
| I smiled | I will smile |
| I laughed | I will laugh |

*Irregular verbs*
I thought
I sang
I ate
I flew

## Expect the unexpected

*Try these...*
Hard    cut, grab, golf, custard, ignite, cabin, grace, sags, code, cape, gust
Soft    range, cell, pages, France, gymnast, grace (soft 'c'), silence, giant, princess

## More about verbs

*Active and passive voice*
1  a) passive
   b) active
   c) active
   d) passive

## Parts of speech – pronouns

*Try these ...*
1. Edward, apple
2. Sophie, TV
3. James
4. Cara and Emily
5. Trousers, the man

*Try it yourself*
1. it
2. you
3. I
4. they
5. she

## Synonyms and antonyms

*Synonym challenge*
a) speed
b) trick
c) quick
d) angry
e) rough
f) error
g) force
h) small
i) loath

*Antonym challenge*
a) dirty
b) found
c) quiet
d) peace
e) enemy
f) early
g) empty
h) short
i) false

## Parts of speech – adjectives

*Try these...*
safer, safest
hotter, hottest
luckier, luckiest
thinner, thinnest
hungrier, hungriest

## Silent letters

*Try it yourself*
gnu, wreck, gnarled, knot, write, gnome, kneel, wrap, wrong, knit, wren, gnash, wriggle, gnat, knuckle, gnaw, wrinkle, knight, wretch

Rule 1 – n
Rule 2 – n
Rule 3 – r

## Parts of speech – adverbs

*Try these...*
1. humble, humbly   noisy, noisily   truthful, truthfully

2a) hurriedly
  b) easily
  c) peacefully

# Answers

## Parts of speech – conjunctions

*Common conjunctions*
1. so
2. because
3. so that
4. before
5. until

*Try it yourself*
1. After she got home, Mrs Barnes took off her coat.
2. While he ate his tea, Mr Green watched television
3. Whenever I have time I visit my uncle
4. As you have been misbehaving, you can't go out.

## Sentences and clauses

*Simple one-clause sentences*

| Subject | Verb |
| --- | --- |
| The pop singer | played |
| The angry dog | barked |
| The sheep | grazed |
| My favourite football team | won |

*Single or double?*
1. one
2. two
3. one
4. two
5. two
6. one

*Try this...*
which
when
who
in case

## Types of text

*Try this...*
1. Firstly (peel) the bananas
2. Then (mash) them with a fork
3. After this, (add) the ice cream and (mix) it in
4. Next (add) the milk and (stir) until the mixture is smooth
5. Following this, (serve) up your milkshakes in glasses
6. Lastly, (put) some 'sprinkles' on top to make it look nice.
7. (Enjoy) your milkshakes with a friend!

## Punctuating speech

So – what have you learned.
'Where are you going with that ball?' my mum asked.
'I'm going into the garden,' I replied.
'What are you going to do?' she asked.
'I'm going to practise heading the ball against the wall,' I answered.
'But the garden's too small!' my mum exclaimed.
'Don't worry. I'll be careful, ' I assured her.
'Make sure you don't head the ball near the windows,' my mother warned.
'I won't, ' I replied with a grin.

## Tricky spellings

*Try this.*

| fit | fitter | fittest | fitting | fitted |
| --- | --- | --- | --- | --- |
| hot | hotter | hottest | | |
| flat | flatter | flattest | | |
| plan | | | planning | planned |
| jog | jogger | | jogging | jogged |
| big | bigger | biggest | | |
| ban | banner | | banning | banned |

## Word-building with affixes

*Try this...*
angle, port. just, friend, control, magic, agree,
clear, sign, suit, free.

*Try these...*

| awful | -ful | awe |
| --- | --- | --- |
| Portuguese | -ese | Portugal |
| wondrous | -ous | wonder |
| ignorant | -ant | ignore |
| argument | -ment | argue |
| roguish | -ish | rogue |
| responsible | -ible | response |
| wisdom | -dom | wise |
| happiness | -ness | happy |
| cyclist | -ist | cycle |
| communication | -tion | communicate |

## Punctuation in words

*Try it yourself*
1. hard-working
2. clean-shaven
3. long-necked
4. passer-by

*Try this*
Ben's card
The lady's hat
The farmer's cow
Mr Shah's case

*Try this...*
The ants' nest
The teachers' car park
The children's book
The deer's antlers

## Parts of speech – prepositions

*Try these*

| q | w | u | p | x | a | r | d | r | e |
|---|---|---|---|---|---|---|---|---|---|
| t | y | p | z | d | o | w | n | a | s |
| a | o | f | f | d | f | g | h | j | k |
| l | m | n | b | v | x | o | v | e | r |
| z | v | u | n | d | e | r | h | g | t |
| w | t | q | r | o | u | n | d | f | g |
| h | b | v | b | e | t | w | e | e | n |
| u | p | o | n | b | h | y | r | w | d |
| q | w | a | b | o | v | e | k | l | j |
| m | n | v | b | e | l | o | w | x | z |

## Spelling rules

*Try this...*
receive
mischief
deceive
relief
yield
receipt
grief

*Try this...*
lorries, supplies
laziness, prettiness
furious, mysterious
wearily, hungrily

noisier, noisiest
heavier, heaviest
busier, busiest

hurries, hurried
relies, relied
multiplies, multiplied

*DIY mnemonics*
1. The bus was busy.
2. Never believe a lie.
3. I would like a piece of pie.
4. You are only young once.
5. I will be friend till the very end.
6. It's great to eat.
7. U an i can build a wall.
8. Don't ride a bicycle in icy weather.

## The history of our language

*Try this...*
boomerang – Australia
café – France
bungalow – India
yacht – Holland
moccasin – North America
reggae – Jamaica
hamburger – Germany
banana – Portugal
chocolate – France
mosque – Egypt
sauna – Finland

*Try it yourself*

| English | Latin |
|---|---|
| anniversary | annus |
| temporary | tempus |
| dental | dentis |
| amiable | amo |
| movement | moveo |
| proverb | verbum |
| abbreviate | brevis |
| manufacture | manus |

# Timetable

| Time | Monday | Tuesday | Wednesday | Thursday | Friday |
|------|--------|---------|-----------|----------|--------|
|      |        |         |           |          |        |
|      |        |         |           |          |        |
|      |        |         |           |          |        |
|      |        |         |           |          |        |
| B R E A K   T I M E | | | | | |
|      |        |         |           |          |        |
|      |        |         |           |          |        |
|      |        |         |           |          |        |
|      |        |         |           |          |        |
| L U N C H   T I M E | | | | | |
|      |        |         |           |          |        |
|      |        |         |           |          |        |
|      |        |         |           |          |        |
| B R E A K   T I M E | | | | | |
|      |        |         |           |          |        |
|      |        |         |           |          |        |
|      |        |         |           |          |        |

# Notes